CURSIVE HANDWRITING WORKBOOK FOR TEENS:

LEARNING CURSIVE WITH INSPIRATIONAL QUOTES

THIS BOOK BELONGS TO :

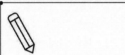

Introduction to Learning cursive

Welcome to *Cursive handwriting workbook for teens: Learning cursive with inspirational quotes*! We are glad to be a part of your journey in learning. Whether you are in your early or late teenage years, or even in your young adulthood, it is never too late to begin learning to write in cursive. Today's technology has all of us virtually doing "written" work on computers or digital gadgets, and this is why it is more common among children of the modern age to grow up falling a little short on penmanship. It is important to know that neuroscientists believe that learning cursive is developmentally beneficial for the human brain, at any stage. Scientific studies have found evidence that the brain is "activated" in meaningful ways when writing in cursive. The main benefit of which is that your levels of fluency (from more focused reading while writing) will naturally be enhanced as you go along. Writing by hand, especially in cursive, is vital in training the brain to practice and, thus improve, more skills and senses all at once: hand-eye coordination, patience, self-control, and a sense of involvement and ownership. All this, while learning more about the English language.

In this book, you will find various writing exercises in small font size designed for teenagers and young adults alike, to help with learning cursive writing. The first part starts off with the alphabet where writing letters in both lowercase and capital forms are practiced through tracing and connecting the dots. Each letter is presented with directional arrows to guide the hand movements as you learn to write. This book has plenty of space with a whole page for practicing each letter.The second part moves on to writing inspirational quotes in cursive from historical people like: Leonardo da Vinci, Abraham Lincoln, Socrates, Queen Victoria, Voltaire and many others. There are two worksheets with exercises for each quote. You will gain thorough practice in writing words first, which are extracted from the quote with a traceable cursive font. The next step moves on to writing the entire sentence from the quote multiple times.

It may seem tedious at first, but trust that cursive handwriting will help establish the tenacity that is important for your many learning experiences throughout life. This book is our tribute to all you teens and young adults who have taken an active part in your continuous cognitive growth!

CURSIVE HANDWRITING WORKBOOK FOR TEENS:

Learning cursive with inspirational quotes

WHAT'S INSIDE?

A FEW TIPS:

Good posture is essential during writing. Sitting upright with feet flat on the floor will help with your writing efficiency.

B Pencils are softer and glides better on paper. You may likewise start practicing cursive writing with ink pens once proficiency with cursive letters has been achieved.

Be conscious of your pencil grip. Always make sure that the pad of the thumb touches your pen for easier, unrestricted writing motions.

Stay patient! Learning cursive writing is a journey of learning and growth. Remember, nothing of real value is ever easy.

CURSIVE WRITING GUIDE

$A\,a$ $B\,b$ $C\,c$ $D\,d$ $E\,e$

$F\,f$ $G\,g$ $H\,h$ $I\,i$ $J\,j$

$K\,k$ $L\,l$ $M\,m$ $N\,n$ $O\,o$

$P\,p$ $Q\,q$ $R\,r$ $S\,s$ $T\,t$

$U\,u$ $V\,v$ $W\,w$ $X\,x$ $Y\,y$

$Z\,z$

Part 1:

Learning Cursive Letters

Trace the dotted letters,
then write the letters on your own.

a a a a a a a

a a a a a a a

a a a a a a a

a a a a a a a

a a a a a a a

a

a

a

a

a

a

a

a

a

a

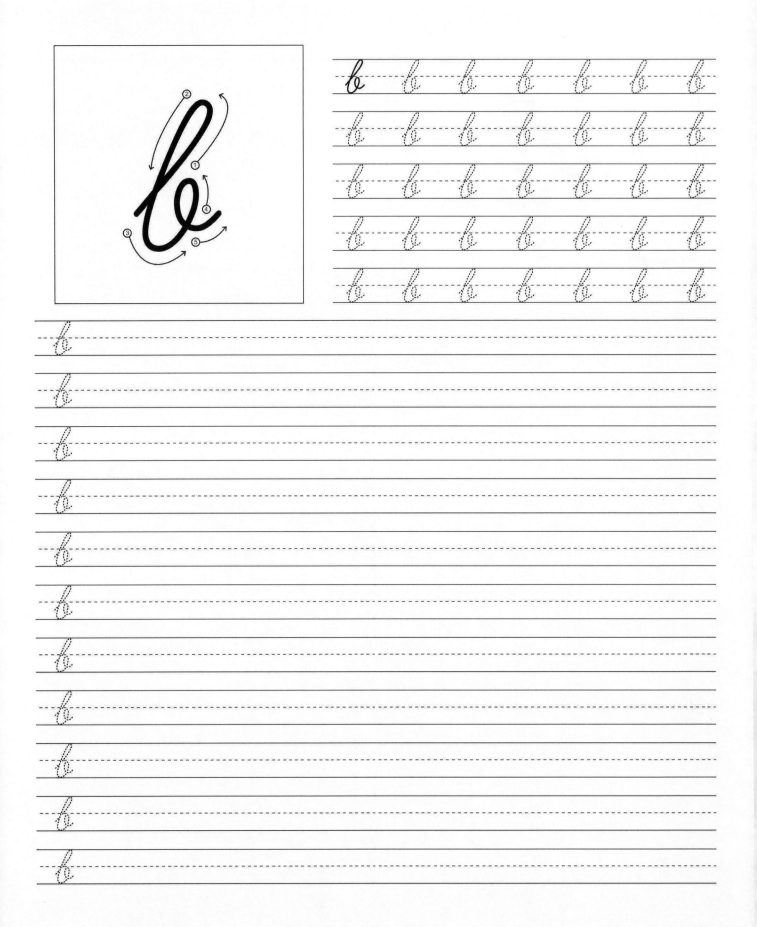

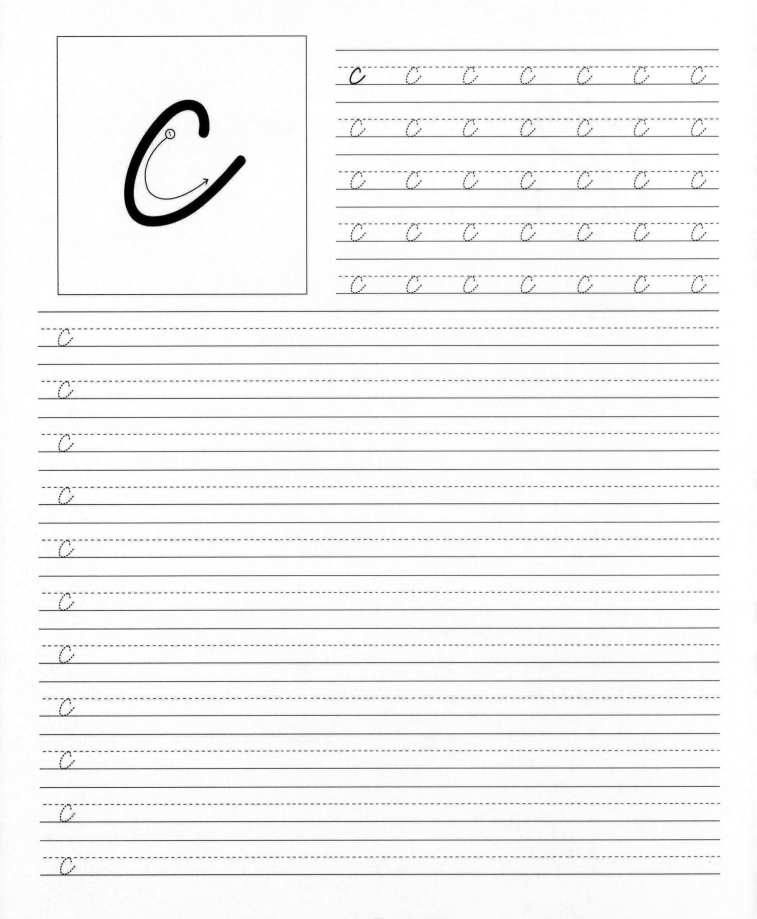

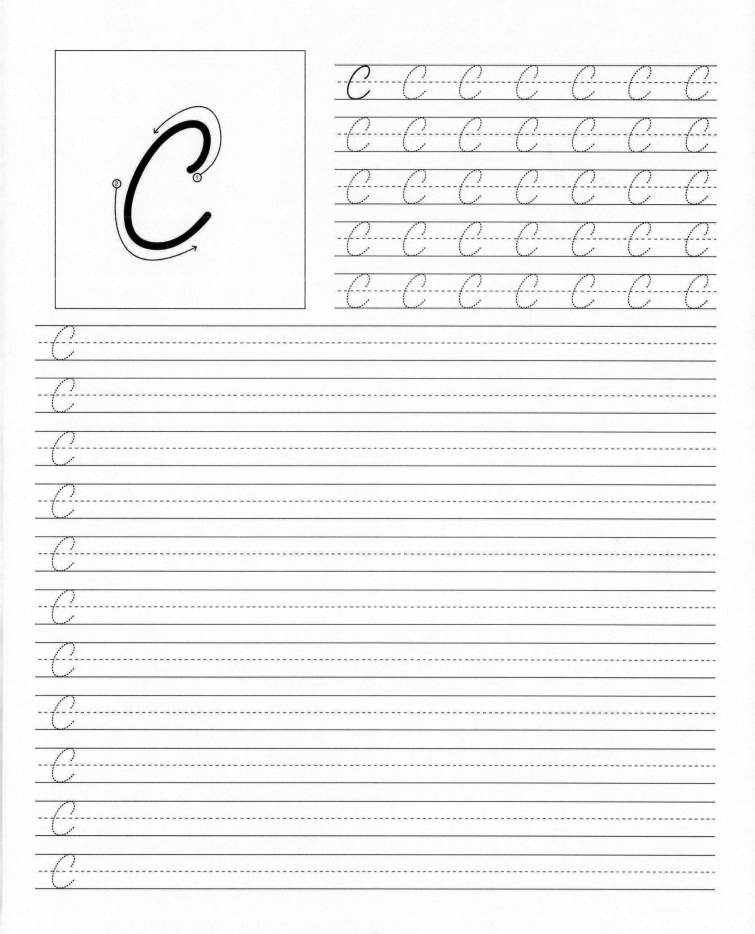

d   d   d   d   d   d   d

d   d   d   d   d   d   d

d   d   d   d   d   d   d

d   d   d   d   d   d   d

d   d   d   d   d   d   d

d

d

d

d

d

d

d

d

d

d

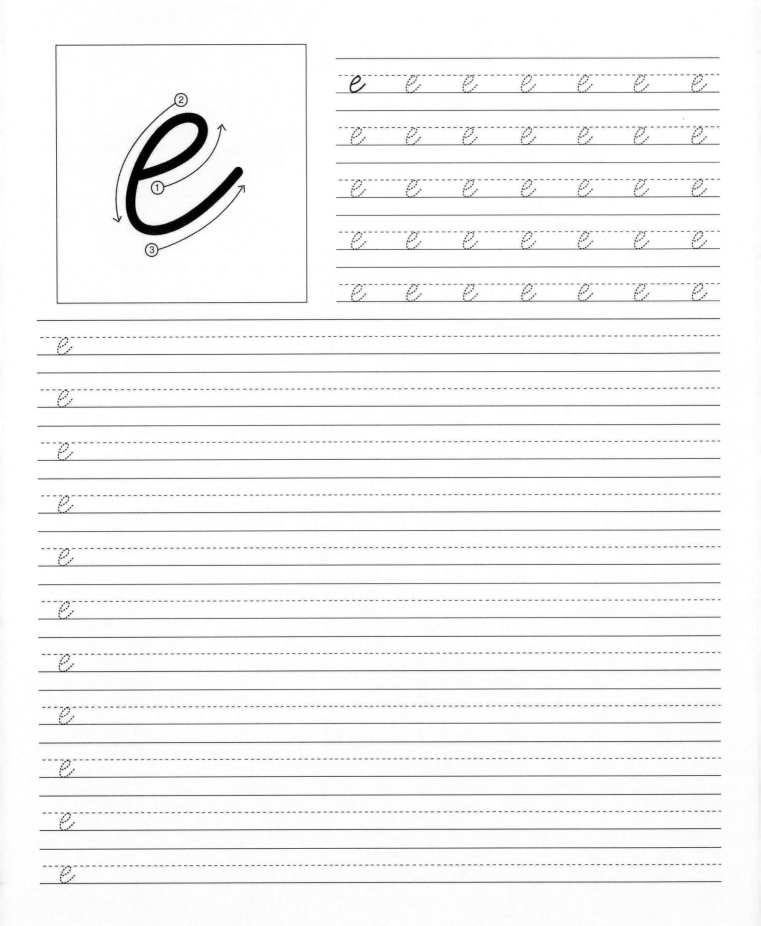

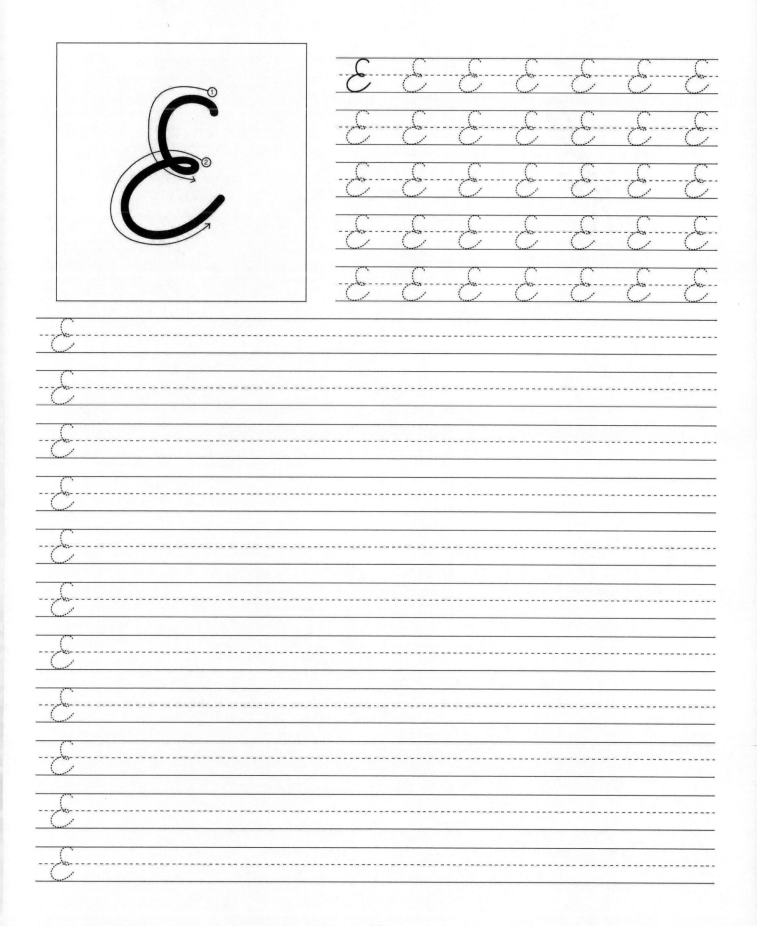

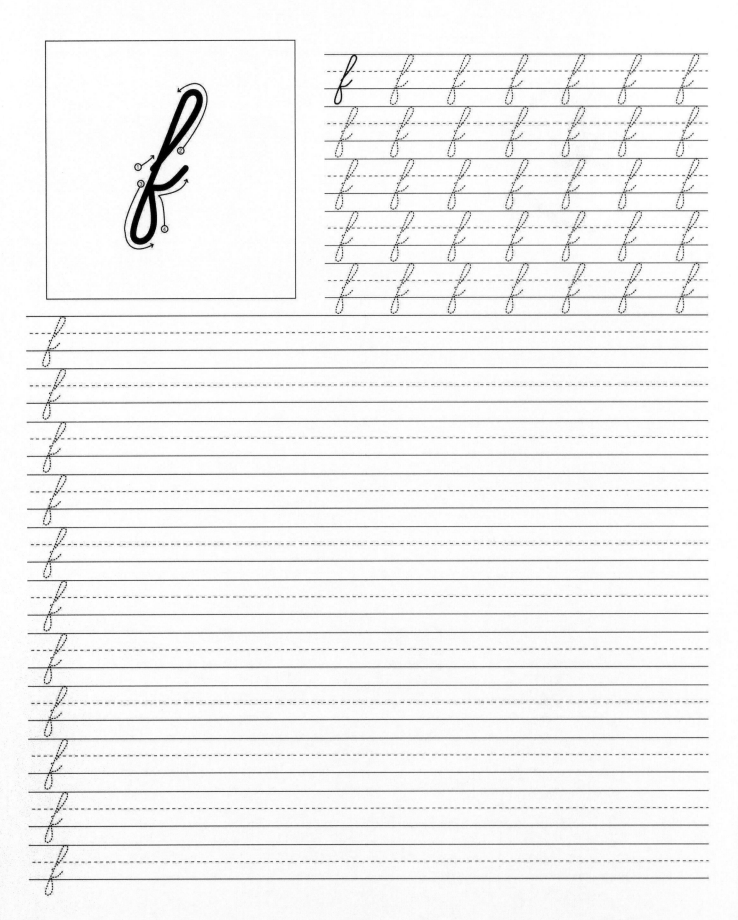

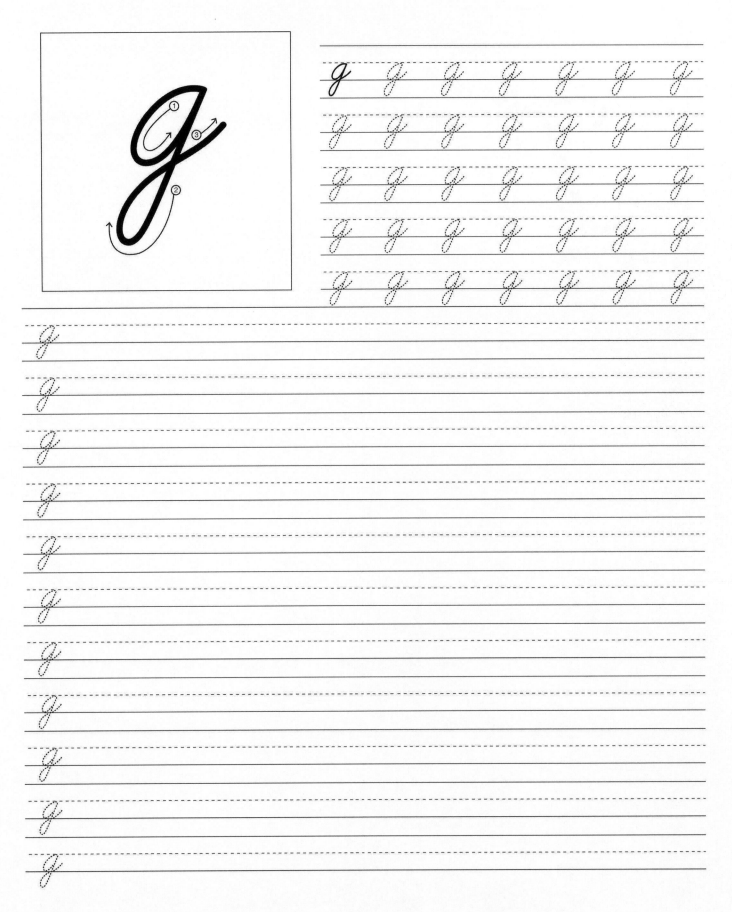

18

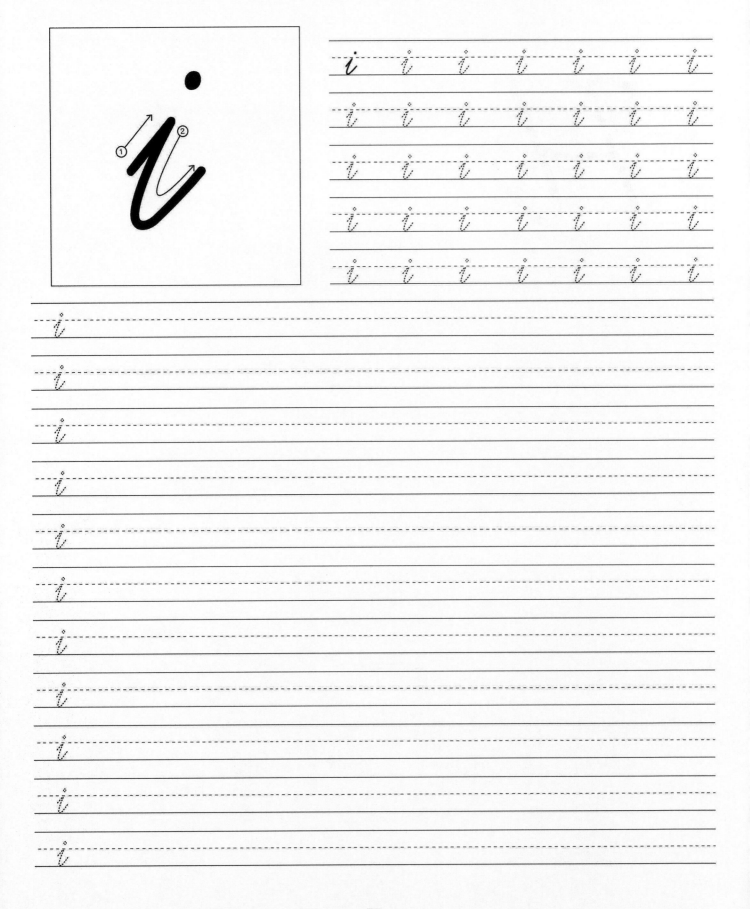

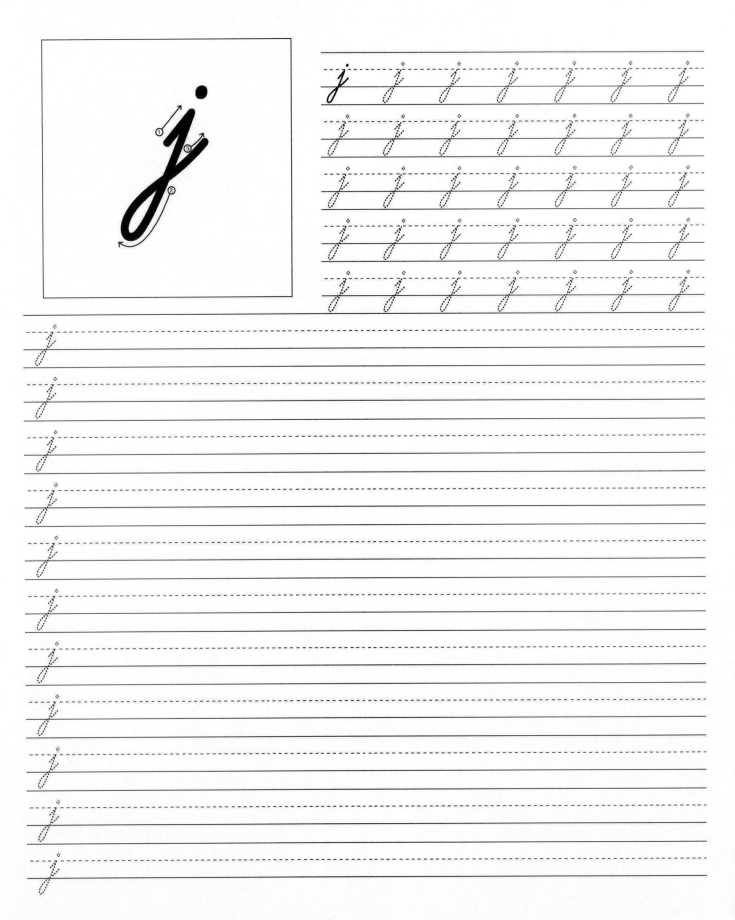

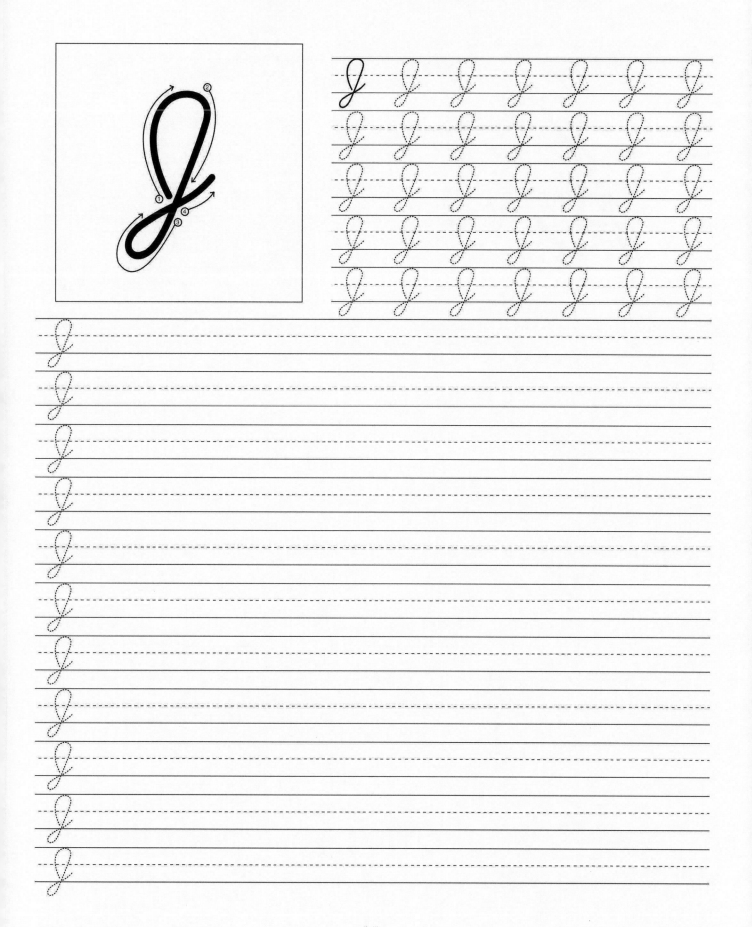

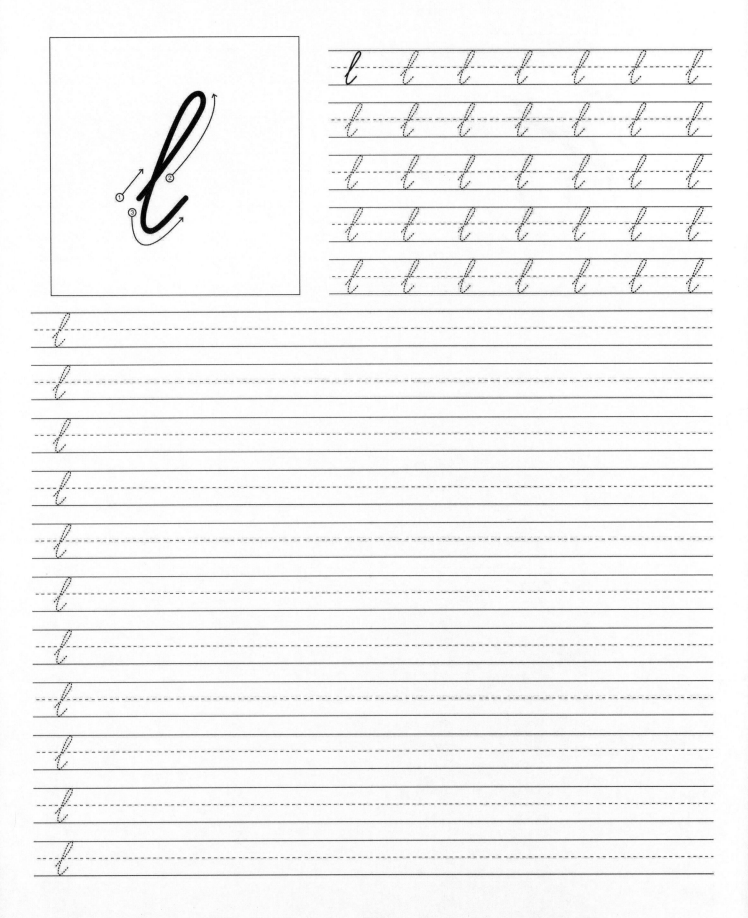

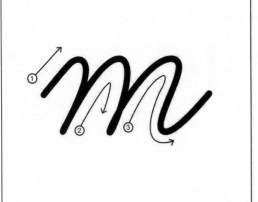

m m m m m m m

m m m m m m m

m m m m m m m

m m m m m m m

m m m m m m m

m

m

m

m

m

m

m

m

m

m

m

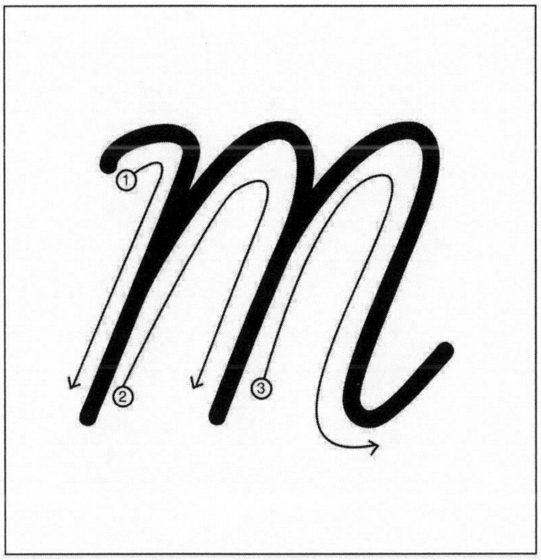
1
2
3

𝑛 𝑛 𝑛 𝑛 𝑛 𝑛 𝑛

𝑛 𝑛 𝑛 𝑛 𝑛 𝑛 𝑛

𝑛 𝑛 𝑛 𝑛 𝑛 𝑛 𝑛

𝑛 𝑛 𝑛 𝑛 𝑛 𝑛 𝑛

𝑛 𝑛 𝑛 𝑛 𝑛 𝑛 𝑛

𝑛

𝑛

𝑛

𝑛

𝑛

𝑛

𝑛

𝑛

𝑛

𝑛

𝑛

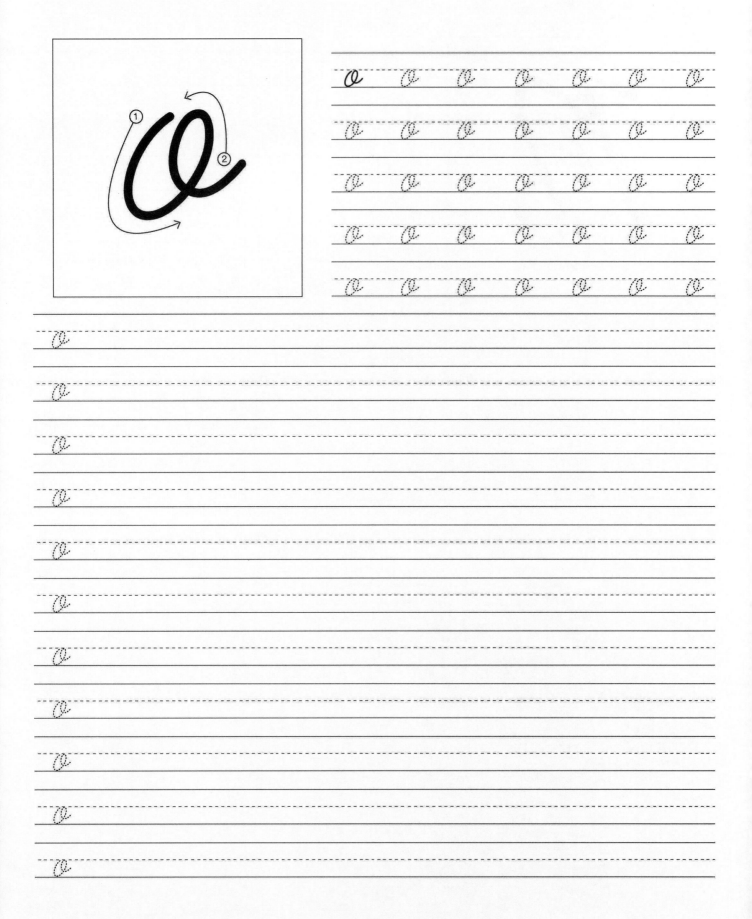

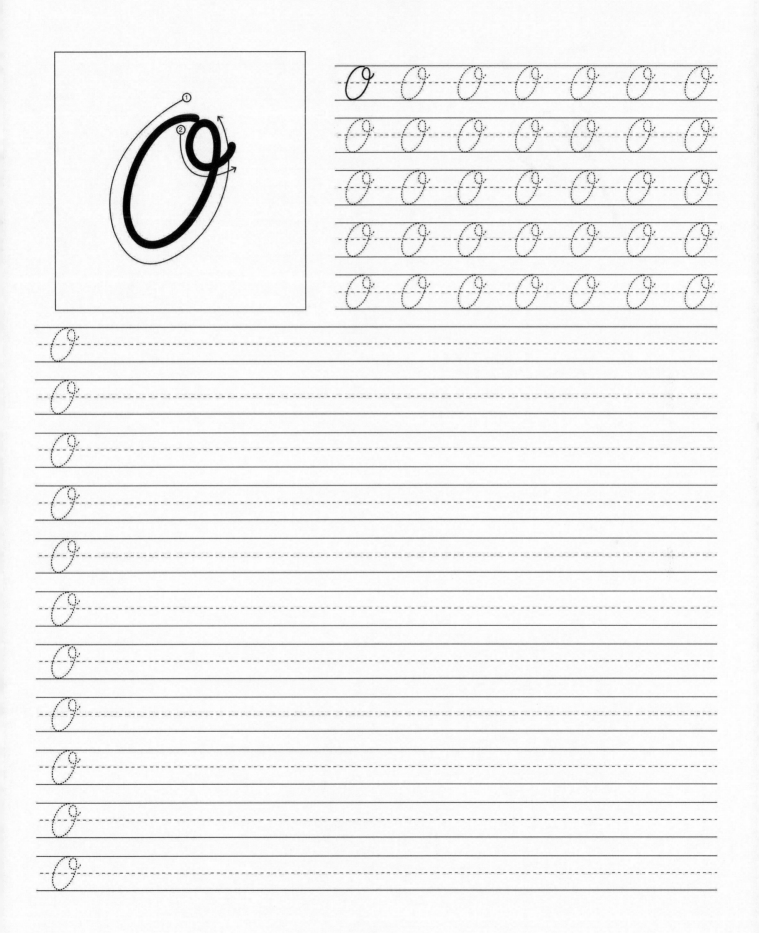

p p p p p p p

p p p p p p p

p p p p p p p

p p p p p p p

p p p p p p p

p

p

p

p

p

p

p

p

p

p

p

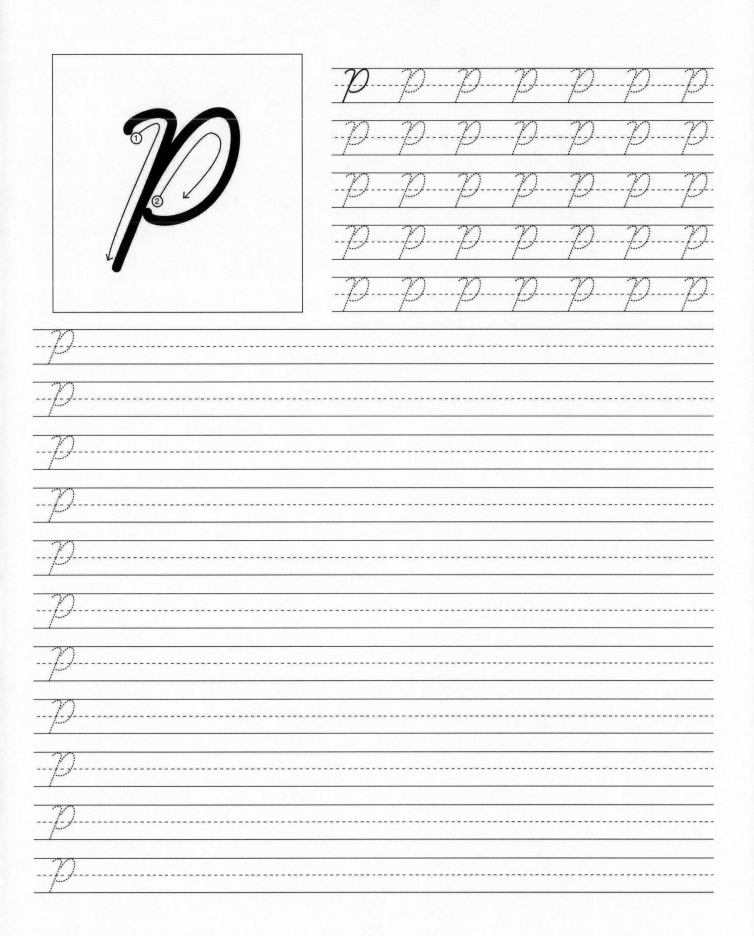

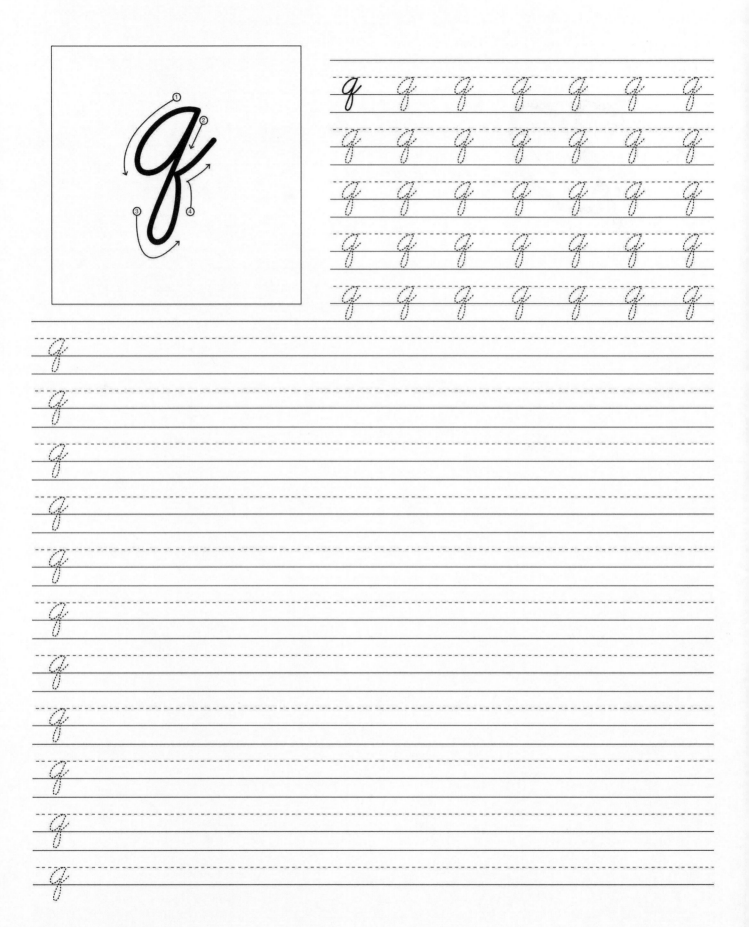

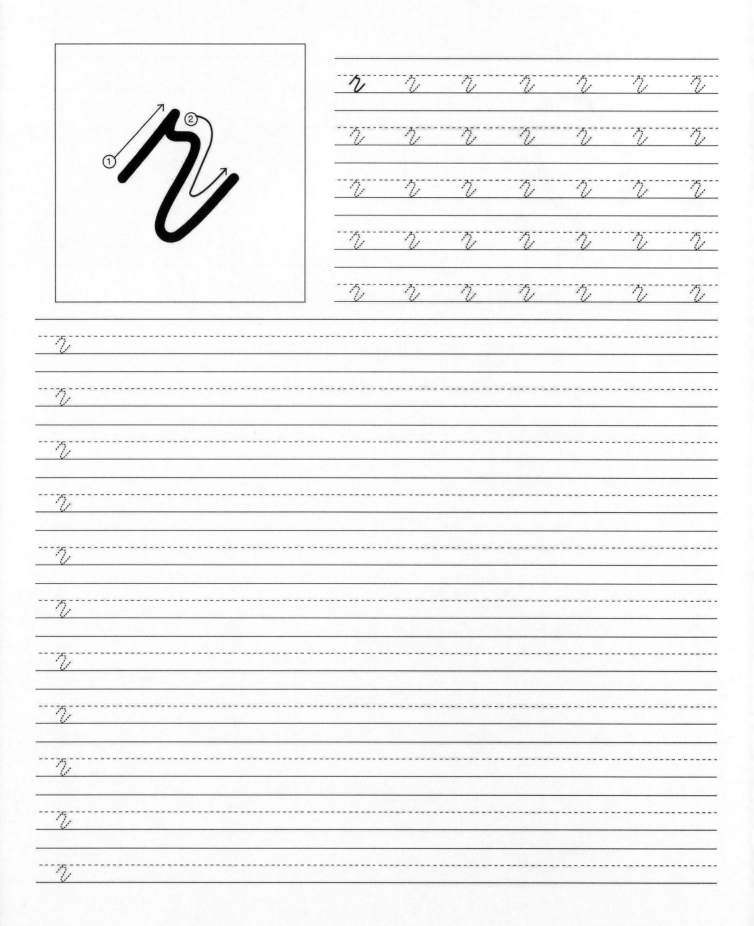

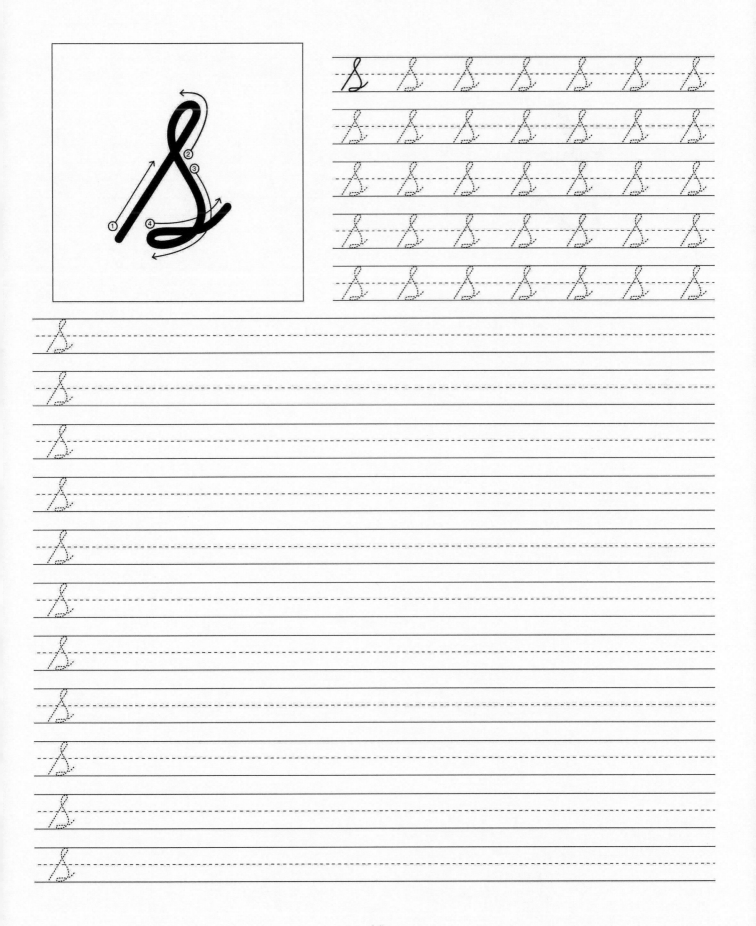

t   t   t   t   t   t   t

t   t   t   t   t   t   t

t   t   t   t   t   t   t

t   t   t   t   t   t   t

t   t   t   t   t   t   t

t

t

t

t

t

t

t

t

t

t

$\mathcal{U}$ $\mathcal{U}$ $\mathcal{U}$ $\mathcal{U}$ $\mathcal{U}$ $\mathcal{U}$ $\mathcal{U}$

$\mathcal{U}$ $\mathcal{U}$ $\mathcal{U}$ $\mathcal{U}$ $\mathcal{U}$ $\mathcal{U}$ $\mathcal{U}$

$\mathcal{U}$ $\mathcal{U}$ $\mathcal{U}$ $\mathcal{U}$ $\mathcal{U}$ $\mathcal{U}$ $\mathcal{U}$

$\mathcal{U}$ $\mathcal{U}$ $\mathcal{U}$ $\mathcal{U}$ $\mathcal{U}$ $\mathcal{U}$ $\mathcal{U}$

$\mathcal{U}$ $\mathcal{U}$ $\mathcal{U}$ $\mathcal{U}$ $\mathcal{U}$ $\mathcal{U}$ $\mathcal{U}$

$\mathcal{U}$

$\mathcal{U}$

$\mathcal{U}$

$\mathcal{U}$

$\mathcal{U}$

$\mathcal{U}$

$\mathcal{U}$

$\mathcal{U}$

$\mathcal{U}$

$\mathcal{U}$

$\mathcal{U}$

43

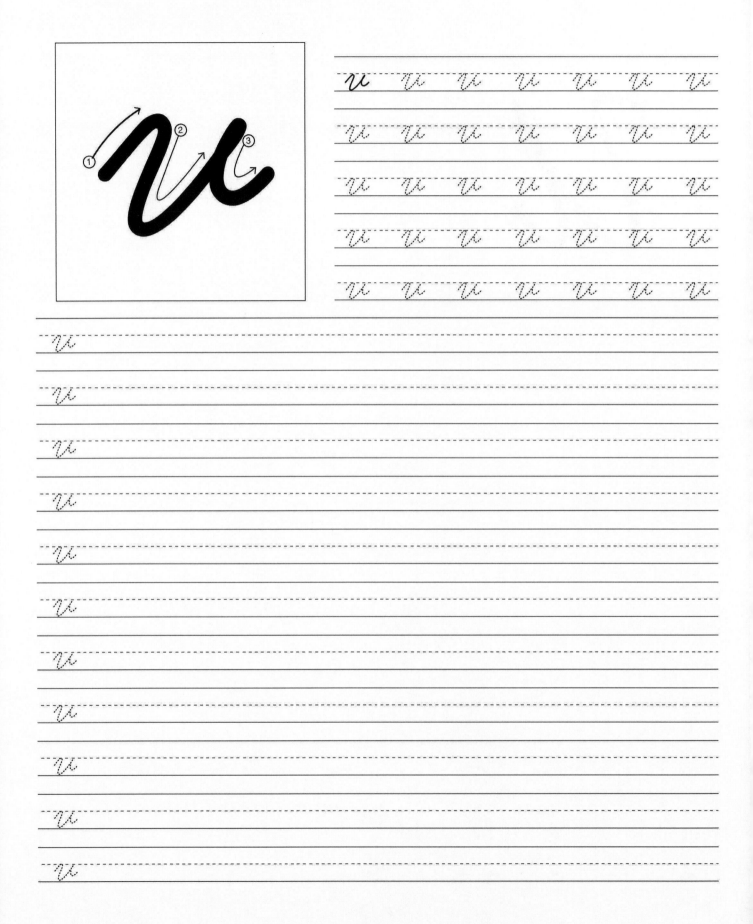

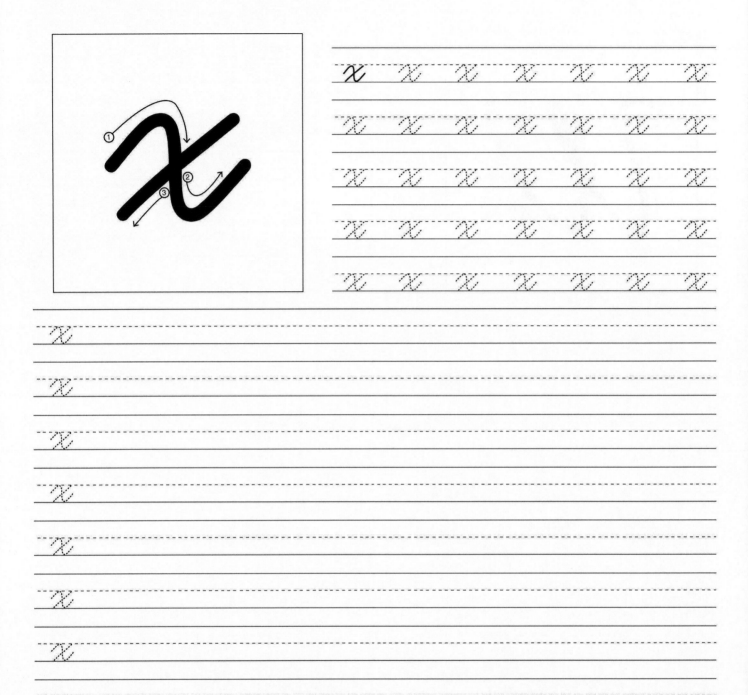

$\mathcal{Y}$

$\mathcal{Y}$ $\mathcal{Y}$ $\mathcal{Y}$ $\mathcal{Y}$ $\mathcal{Y}$ $\mathcal{Y}$ $\mathcal{Y}$

$\mathcal{Y}$ $\mathcal{Y}$ $\mathcal{Y}$ $\mathcal{Y}$ $\mathcal{Y}$ $\mathcal{Y}$ $\mathcal{Y}$

$\mathcal{Y}$ $\mathcal{Y}$ $\mathcal{Y}$ $\mathcal{Y}$ $\mathcal{Y}$ $\mathcal{Y}$ $\mathcal{Y}$

$\mathcal{Y}$ $\mathcal{Y}$ $\mathcal{Y}$ $\mathcal{Y}$ $\mathcal{Y}$ $\mathcal{Y}$ $\mathcal{Y}$

$\mathcal{Y}$ $\mathcal{Y}$ $\mathcal{Y}$ $\mathcal{Y}$ $\mathcal{Y}$ $\mathcal{Y}$ $\mathcal{Y}$

$\mathcal{Y}$

$\mathcal{Y}$

$\mathcal{Y}$

$\mathcal{Y}$

$\mathcal{Y}$

$\mathcal{Y}$

$\mathcal{Y}$

$\mathcal{Y}$

$\mathcal{Y}$

$\mathcal{Y}$

$\mathcal{Y}$

55

Part 2:

Learning cursive words and sentences with inspirational quotes

Trace the dotted words and sentences, then write them on your own.

"Wonder is the beginning of wisdom."

−Socrates

Wonder   Wonder

is   is

the   the

beginning   beginning

of   of

wisdom   wisdom

Wonder is the beginning of wisdom.

Wonder is the beginning of wisdom.

"Experience is the teacher of all things."

−Julius Caesar

Experience Experience

is is

the the

teacher teacher

of of

all things all things

Experience is the teacher of all things.

Experience is the teacher of all things.

"There is no substitute for hard work."
-Thomas A. Edison

There   There

is   is

no   no

substitute   substitute

for   for

hard work   hard work

There is no substitute for hard work.

There is no substitute for hard work.

"Diligence is the mother of good luck."
– Benjamin Franklin

Diligence Diligence

is is

the mother the mother

of of

good good

luck luck

Diligence is the mother of good luck.

Diligence is the mother of good luck.

"Education is the best provision for old age."

– Aristotle

Education   Education

is   is

the best   the best

provision   provision

for   for

old age   old age

Education is the best provision for old age.

Education is the best provision for old age.

"Be the change that you wish to see in the world."
- Mahatma Gandhi

Be the change Be the change

that you that you

wish wish

to see to see

in in

the world the world

Be the change that you wish to see in
the world.

Be the change that you wish to see in
the world.

"*Before anything else, preparation is the key to success.*"
— Alexander Graham Bell

Before anything *Before anything*

else *else*

preparation *preparation*

is the *is the*

key *key*

to success *to success*

Before anything else, preparation is the key to success.

Before anything else, preparation is the key to success.

"The journey of a thousand miles begins with one step."

–Lao Tzu

The journey   *The journey*

of a thousand   *of a thousand*

miles   *miles*

begins   *begins*

with   *with*

one step   *one step*

The journey of a thousand miles begins with one step.

The journey of a thousand miles begins with one step.

"Every man is guilty of all the good he didn't do."

–Voltaire

Every man   Every man

is   is

guilty   guilty

of all the   of all the

good   good

he didn't do   he didn't do

Every man is guilty of all the good
he didn't do.

Every man is guilty of all the good
he didn't do.

"Never interrupt your enemy when he is making a mistake."
–Napoleon Bonaparte

Never interrupt   Never interrupt

your enemy   your enemy

when   when

he is   he is

making   making

a mistake   a mistake

Never interrupt your enemy when he
is making a mistake.

*Never interrupt your enemy when he
is making a mistake.*

"The ideal friendship is to feel as one while remaining two."
—Sophie Swetchine

The ideal

friendship

is to feel

as one

while

remaining two

The ideal friendship is to feel as one while remaining two.

The ideal friendship is to feel as one while remaining two.

"I cannot teach anybody anything.
I can only make them think."
– Socrates

I cannot teach   I cannot teach

anybody   anybody

anything   anything

I can only   I can only

make   make

them think   them think

I cannot teach anybody anything.

I can only make them think.

I cannot teach anybody anything.

I can only make them think.

"It does not matter how slowly you go as long as you do not stop."
–Confucius

It does not   It does not

matter how   matter how

slowly you   slowly you

go as long   go as long

as you do   as you do

not stop   not stop

It does not matter how slowly you go
as long as you do not stop.

It does not matter how slowly you go
as long as you do not stop.

"It is far better to be alone, than to be in bad company."
– George Washington

It is far better   It is far better

to be alone   to be alone

than   than

to be   to be

in bad   in bad

company   company

It is far better to be alone, than to be in bad company.

It is far better to be alone, than to be in bad company.

"A room without books is like a body without a soul."
– Marcus Tullius Cicero

A room   A room

without   without

books is   books is

like a   like a

body without   body without

a soul   a soul

A room without books is like a body

without a soul.

A room without books is like a body

without a soul.

"We will not have failure – only success
and new learning."
–Queen Victoria

We will not   We will not

have failure   have failure

only success   only success

and   and

new   new

learning   learning

We will not have failure — only success
and new learning.

We will not have failure — only success
and new learning.

"I find that the harder I work, the more luck I seem to have."
-Thomas Jefferson

I find that I find that

the harder I work the harder I work

the more the more

luck luck

I seem I seem

to have to have

I find that the harder I work, the more
luck I seem to have.

I find that the harder I work, the more
luck I seem to have.

"Friends show their love in times
of trouble, not in happiness."
-Euripides

Friends show their   Friends show their

love in   love in

times   times

of trouble   of trouble

not   not

in happiness   in happiness

Friends show their love in times of
trouble, not in happiness.

Friends show their love in times of
trouble, not in happiness.

> "I hear and I forget. I see and I remember. I do and I understand."
>
> –Confucius

I hear and   I hear and

I forget   I forget

I see and   I see and

I remember   I remember

I do and   I do and

I understand   I understand

I hear and I forget. I see and I remember. I do and I understand.

I hear and I forget. I see and I remember. I do and I understand.

"One can have no smaller or greater mastery than mastery of oneself."
–Leonardo da Vinci

One can have   One can have

no smaller or   no smaller or

greater mastery   greater mastery

than mastery   than mastery

of   of

oneself   oneself

One can have no smaller or greater
mastery than mastery of oneself.
One can have no smaller or greater
mastery than mastery of oneself.

"The present is theirs ; the future, for which I really worked, is mine."
– Nikola Tesla

The present   The present

is theirs   is theirs

the future   the future

for which   for which

I really worked   I really worked

is mine   is mine

The present is theirs; the future, for which
I really worked, is mine.

The present is theirs; the future, for which
I really worked, is mine.

"The work of today is the history of tomorrow, and we are its makers."
–Juliette Gordon Low

The work of today

is the history

of tomorrow

and

we are its

makers

The work of today is the history of
tomorrow, and we are its makers.

The work of today is the history of
tomorrow, and we are its makers.

"I am not afraid of storms, for I am learning how to sail my ship."
– Louisa May Alcott

I am not afraid   I am not afraid

of storms   of storms

for I am   for I am

learning how   learning how

to sail   to sail

my ship   my ship

I am not afraid of storms, for I am
learning how to sail my ship.

I am not afraid of storms, for I am
learning how to sail my ship.

"There is nothing on this earth more to be prized than true friendship."
–Thomas Aquinas

There is nothing   There is nothing

on this earth   on this earth

more to be   more to be

prized than   prized than

true   true

friendship   friendship

There is nothing on this earth more to be
prized than true friendship.

There is nothing on this earth more to be
prized than true friendship.

"Tell me and I forget. Teach me and I remember. Involve me and I learn."
-Benjamin Franklin

Tell me and   Tell me and

I forget   I forget

Teach me and   Teach me and

I remember   I remember

Involve me   Involve me

and I learn   and I learn

Tell me and I forget. Teach me and I remember. Involve me and I learn.

Tell me and I forget. Teach me and I remember. Involve me and I learn.

"Success usually comes to those who
are too busy to be looking for it."
–Henry David Thoreau

Success usually   *Success usually*

comes to those   *comes to those*

who are too   *who are too*

busy to be   *busy to be*

looking   *looking*

for it   *for it*

Success usually comes to those who are
too busy to be looking for it.

Success usually comes to those who are
too busy to be looking for it.

"Study without desire spoils the memory, and it retains nothing that it takes in."

—Leonardo da Vinci

Study without *Study without*

desire spoils *desire spoils*

the memory *the memory*

and it retains *and it retains*

nothing that *nothing that*

it takes in *it takes in*

Study without desire spoils the memory,
and it retains nothing that it takes in.

Study without desire spoils the memory,
and it retains nothing that it takes in.

"As I grow older, I pay less attention to what men say. I just watch what they do."
– Andrew Carnegie

As I grow older   As I grow older

I pay less attention   I pay less attention

to what men say   to what men say

I just   I just

watch what   watch what

they do   they do

As I grow older, I pay less attention to what men say. I just watch what they do.

As I grow older, I pay less attention to what men say. I just watch what they do.

"First they ignore you, then they laugh at you, then they fight you, then you win."
-Mahatma Gandhi

First they ignore *First they ignore*

you, then they *you, then they*

laugh at you, *laugh at you,*

then they fight *then they fight*

you, then *you, then*

you win *you win*

First they ignore you, then they laugh at you, then they fight you, then you win.

First they ignore you, then they laugh at you, then they fight you, then you win.

"Don't judge each day by the harvest
that you reap but by the seeds
that you plant."
– Robert Louis Stevenson

Don't judge each   *Don't judge each*

day by the harvest   *day by the harvest*

that you reap   *that you reap*

but by   *but by*

the seeds   *the seeds*

that you plant   *that you plant*

Don't judge each day by the harvest that
you reap but by the seeds that you plant.
Don't judge each day by the harvest that
you reap but by the seeds that you plant.

"The greatest test of courage on earth is to bear defeat without losing heart."
–Robert Green Ingersoll

The greatest   *The greatest*

test of courage   *test of courage*

on earth is to   *on earth is to*

bear defeat   *bear defeat*

without   *without*

losing heart   *losing heart*

The greatest test of courage on earth is
to bear defeat without losing heart.

The greatest test of courage on earth is
to bear defeat without losing heart.

*"The World is my country,
all mankind are my brethren, and to
do good is my religion."*
—Thomas Paine

The World is my   The World is my

country, all   country, all

mankind are my   mankind are my

brethren and to   brethren and to

do good is my   do good is my

religion   religion

The World is my country, all mankind
are my brethren, and to do good is my
religion.

The World is my country, all mankind
are my brethren, and to do good is my
religion.

"Very little is needed to make a happy
life; it is all within yourself,
in your way of thinking."
—Marcus Aurelius

Very little is

needed to make

a happy life

it is all within

yourself, in your

way of thinking

Very little is needed to make a happy life; it is all within yourself, in your way of thinking.

Very little is needed to make a happy life; it is all within yourself, in your way of thinking.

"Wise men speak because they have something to say; Fools because they have to say something."

–Plato

Wise men speak

Wise men speak

because they have

because they have

something to say

something to say

Fools because they

Fools because they

have to

have to

say something

say something

Wise men speak because they have something to say; Fools because they have to say something.

Wise men speak because they have something to say; Fools because they have to say something.

"If your actions inspire others to dream more, learn more, do more and become more, you are a leader."

−John Quincy Adams

If your actions

inspire others

to dream more

learn more, do more

and become more

you are a leader

If your actions inspire others to dream more, learn more, do more and become more, you are a leader.

If your actions inspire others to dream more, learn more, do more and become more, you are a leader.

"I don't know who my grandfather was;
I am much more concerned to know
what his grandson will be."
– Abraham Lincoln

I don't know who   I don't know who

my grandfather was   my grandfather was

I am much more   I am much more

concerned to know   concerned to know

what his   what his

grandson will be   grandson will be

I don't know who my grandfather was,
I am much more concerned to know
what his grandson will be.
I don't know who my grandfather was,
I am much more concerned to know
what his grandson will be.

"When everything seems to be going against you, remember that the airplane takes off against the wind, not with it."
–Henry Ford

When everything   *When everything*

seems to be going   *seems to be going*

against you   *against you*

remember that the   *remember that the*

airplane takes off   *airplane takes off*

against the wind, not with it
against the wind, not with it

When everything seems to be going
against you, remember that the airplane
takes off against the wind, not with it.
When everything seems to be going
against you, remember that the airplane
takes off against the wind, not with it.

"When you arise in the morning, think of what a precious privilege it is to be alive — to breathe, to think, to enjoy, to love."

-Marcus Aurelius

When you arise in

the morning, think

of what a precious

privilege it is to be

alive-to breathe,

to think, to enjoy, to love

When you arise in the morning, think of
what a precious privilege it is to be alive
— to breathe, to think, to enjoy, to love.

When you arise in the morning, think of
what a precious privilege it is to be alive
— to breathe, to think, to enjoy, to love.

"All truth passes through three stages. First,
it is ridiculed. Second, it is violently opposed.
Third, it is accepted as being self-evident."
– Arthur Schopenhauer

All truth passes

through three stages

First, it is ridiculed

Second, it is violently
violently

opposed. Third it is

accepted as being self-evident

All truth passes through three stages.
First, it is ridiculed. Second, it is violently
opposed. Third, it is accepted as being
self-evident.

All truth passes through three stages.
First, it is ridiculed. Second, it is violently
opposed. Third, it is accepted as being
self-evident.

"The biggest reward for a thing well done is to have done it."

–Voltaire

The biggest   The biggest

reward for   reward for

a thing   a thing

well done   well done

is to have   is to have

done it   done it

The biggest reward for a thing well done
is to have done it.

The biggest reward for a thing well done is to have done it.

Hi there! Learning cursive with inspirational quotes is a book that was created with YOU in mind: a pre- to young adult who has decided to embark on the journey of learning to write in cursive. We hope that we were able to help you learn cursive writing in an engaging and meaningful way. We would love to hear about it as you write a short review on Amazon for us. Your comments and ideas will help us to develop more educational and interesting books that will help a million other young adults like you!

If you have any questions about this workbook, please feel free to contact Leslie Mars at lesliemarsbooks@gmail.com.